CROWNED

Poems by
JASMINE "QUEEN JASMEEN" SCHLAFKE

Crowned

Jasmine "Queen Jasmeen" Schlafke

Thank you to everyone who worked on this book.

Special thanks to Samantha Berlant, Billy Butler, Stuart Rodriguez, Eric Weinblatt, and Alyssa Young.

Thank you to Chris 'L7' Cuadrado for this book's cover art.

Thank you to Arts Council Santa Cruz County for a grant which supported the printing of this book.

To Jamon and Janessa,
I love you a bushel and a peck.

To Honeysun: rest in power.

Table of Contents

Professional Credentials   1
Human Bio   3
Short Poem on Queendom   4

I. Coronation

Prayer for Coronation   8
1989   9
Untitled (Ferguson)   11
BART   12
Alley Cat   14
Universe Dust   20
Belly   23
Permission   24
Love Letters to My Limbs   26
Interview 1   28
Affirmation for Coronation   31

II. Why I'm Crazy

Prayer for Why I'm Crazy   35
In the Body   36
Bipolar 1: Dear Mom   38
Bipolar 2: Dear Children   40
Bipolar 3: Dear Lovers   42
Underwater   44
Recipe   48
The Black Body   50
Yemaya   52
Affirmation for Why I'm Crazy   55

III. Kinship

Prayer for Kinship	59
My Friend	62
Enough	65
In California	68
Interview 2	71
Confinement Is Timeless	74
Affirmation for Kinship	77

IV. Conclusion

She's Changing Me	80

Jasmine Schlafke: Professional Credentials

Poetry and Theater

Jasmine "Queen Jasmeen" Schlafke trained as an actress at the New Conservatory Theater in San Francisco throughout her childhood and into adolescence. She was nurtured by a family and community of theater, growing up surrounded by set and prop designers, stage directors, writers, and actors. She began to write at the age of twelve and developed herself into the poet and performer she is today. Jasmine started performing competitively in 2011 in the Santa Cruz City Legendary Slam and by 2012 began a winning streak, taking the Santa Cruz Grand Slam Championship three years in a row, including the San Jose Championship in 2014. As an adult, she has worked with Rainbow Theater (UCSC) and Pisces Moon Theater Company.

Public Speaking, Education, and Consulting

Jasmine Schlafke works as an educator, public speaker, and diversity consultant throughout the community, ranging from local grassroots and non-profit organizations to community college and university campuses. She has worked in alternative school settings, where she has developed empowerment skills in at-risk[1] youth and youth of color from low-income communities by teaching writing and performance poetry. Her workshops include: Practical Magic in Writing: Writing as Spiritual Practice, Revolutionary Secret Sharing, Social Justice as Personal Narrative, and Sexual Silence No More.

---

1 *Youth of Color who are "at risk" are at risk of becoming entangled in a system of punishment and exploitation by virtue of a social order that criminalizes and dispossess them daily.*

In 2014, Jasmine spoke at TEDx Santa Cruz, on the subject of Creative Resistance as Activism. She explored how art is an expression and extension of activism and a method of resistance to oppression in her body and the spaces she occupies. She was also a student-selected guest performer for Practical Activism, a student run conference committed to social justice.

Jasmine provides diversity training and cultural competency consultation for various organizations. For nine years, she has been a diversity consultant for Common Vision, which specializes in working with inner-city youth and youth of color. She has also provided counseling for Planned Parenthood, the Santa Cruz Women's Health Center, and Santa Cruz City Schools on trans and queer client inclusion.

Jasmine has over two decades of non-profit community experience. From 1996 to 1997, she was a Youth Outreach Worker for the Santa Cruz AIDS Project where she taught sex education in local schools and distributed information about STIs. From 1997 to 1999, she also served as Youth Assistant for the State of California Employment Development Department in Capitola, California. Here, she developed workshops, case management, and peer counseling. From 2005 to 2006, Jasmine was a Coordinator and Educator for the Santa Cruz AIDS Project, where she trained volunteers, performed client intake, and expanded on her AIDS and STI education within the community. She is a recipient of the National Jefferson Award for Public Service.

Human Bio

I am human
I am Love
I am a woman
I am a mother
I live with bipolar disorder,
schizoaffective disorder,
post-traumatic stress disorder
and an anxiety disorder.
I am not disordered.
I am Black.
I am multiracial.
I am a Schlafke.
I am a nomad.
Soy mujer.
I am a dyke-identified bisexual or pansexual depending on
who's deciding.
I am my own decision.
I am a witch.
Soy bruja.
I am part of the struggle
the hustle
the balancing act of survival.

I am human
I am Love
I am a mother
I am a woman

Short Poem on Queendom

Dedicated to the poet who needs to write a fucking book.

Dear Jasmine,

Worthy peasants like you have long enough
called themselves names,
drunk from the pool of bullshit offered by Uncle Sam
in an attempt to hydrate,
stamped themselves unworthy.
So why not be a Queen?
Why not affirm the lion's roar placed in your throat?
The leadership you cannot help but offer?
Why not believe yourself holy?
Meet the world with the understanding that everyone is royal.
So many Black children have seen themselves slave
bent and shackled for the Masters of their captivity.
You know them royal.
You know them worthy.
You are them.
Go back in time and call yourself princess 'til you see your name
sprout from the concrete of your history;
QUEEN JASMEEN
'cause you are a sorcerer who can bleed for days and not die.
You have a bowl in the middle of your pelvis ready to hold
fresh fruits in harvest, if you wish,
'cause you are a mother.
God passed through your body twice
and chose you a worthy home
because you know what it is to survive yourself and still smile,
because the caste system is sick
and you will not collude with illness,
because your ancestors have always sung to you
about your divinity,
because you will be an ancestor one day,
because only some of us know how to feel
rich with no money,
full with no food,
gifted with no gifts.

Yes, affirm your Queendom,
Beloved, with the vigor you hope your kin will for themselves
and live in the Kingdom built of village.
Blessed be this woman named Jasmine whose pen
has a story to tell,
whose narrative is hers and hers alone.
Blessed be the kaleidoscope of her vision,
how she learns and perceives like no other.
Holy be this moment in time when Yes swelled in her heart so
big she could only show up.
Holy be the support that encircles her.
Holy be her
her broken
her trauma
her testimony
her writing
Yes, write a fucking book, Jasmine,
Amen.

Credit to Scheri Lovedog
Photo from The Jesus Factor

I
Coronation

To my revolutionary mother,
Valeria Schlafke

Prayer for Coronation

Beloved Creator,
I trust that I exist within you,
I trust that my design is meant to be supported and this day
pray for my highest good.
That I am part of life itself on purpose and by design.
I bring the all of me I am aware of to your ever-capable hands,
My shame and pride,
My fear and wonder.
I seek this day not to fragment or splinter but to unfold.
Use me for good, for truth, for honesty, for creativity, for justice,
and for LOVE.
I will practice these qualities with myself as I learn to treat
myself as part of you.
I claim healing now as birthright and I give thanks for
an opportunity to pray.
Thank you for my ever-capable body, the tools I know how
to use, and those that are coming,
For my children and testimony,
For my hope even in the midst.
I gladly release this word, trusting you can hold it.
I remember my ancestors and angels are with me right now.
And So It Is
Amen
Ashe

1989

By 1989 I had watched women run to the middle of the street
with their rosaries, through my window, countless times.
But when the earth quaked
there was something different about their jet towards God.
There was purpose in their frantic footsteps
while Gaia rocked and rolled them, they prayed louder
than the crashing glass and reminded the barrio
that Jesus himself hadn't forgot about the Mission.

My neighborhood, it's called the Mission District
of the City of San Francisco.
Forever, it is simply my hood.
And in the years since the earthquake
it has been changed something good
more than rebuilding the rubble
gentrification slowly renamed the hood "worthy."
Know there are prayers bigger than zoning laws and city limits
police jurisdictions and school tax accreditation.
These oraciones delivered in crisis,
the calling out of too many Santos
whispered and yelled by the people
yes, us with wet fronts, strong backs, and regulated sides.
Pray over our concrete still.

During the Día De Los Muertos procession
some say women still run out into the streets
moving their hands like crosses over their fronts
smudging in billows of sage smoke
making their shoes disappear
along with any illusion this isn't sacred land.
Crying elders and vigilant adults attending front porch altars,
unbroken tiny bottles of tequila for someone's good drunk uncle,
children spinning smiles and noises I always translated into,
"We are alive."

All of this
parting the illusion that streets create.
Magic making isn't seasonal here, like brown work.
24th Street whispers who she is,
boycotting grapes at 5 A.M.,
she held her own noise regulations,
mandated gritas when the Niners won,
parades for every quince,
the smell of starch on vatos who weren't too good to walk
a viejita across the street ,
pan dulce pumping perfume over the stench of nasty
embedded into our walkways,
UFW offices in over-crowded split Victorians,
fresh elote smothered with crema fresca,
tamarindo in plastic spoons,
chile on everything,
half-naked Samba dancers and over-dressed mariachis for Carnival,
40s in bolsas the color of our skin.

In every sense, I remember the hood before earthquake
and bureaucratic sin.

Untitled (Ferguson)

No indictment hits Ferguson
and my son can, for the first time at sixteen
now admit mom's ranting on racism makes sense,
at least a little.
This boy, all made up of *Yes, We Can*,
hope inscribed into his retinas,
this prayer of blood grasping for a chance at the American dream.
"You were right, Mom," he says,
as though his knowing blocked the light out of the sky.
This is not the right I've longed for.

No indictment hits Ferguson and I learn a new gratitude
Thank you for my light-skinned son.
Part of me dies in this thought,
this thought, just survival speaking.

My son all spotted white owl,
my body a fundraiser for his life.
Police men are taunting our wombs,
shooting us into submission,
and a part of me dies in this thought.

My son recedes his position
stands on land screaming
"Nigga please,"
they still coming,
you still running.
You have in all ways been
enough drops to be disposable.

And all the Black boys mourn
And all the mothers pray.

BART

In a country where we write songs
about blood-splattered flags
in the dawn's early night,
and re-sing them for everything
from funerals to baseball games,
does death even faze you?

There was a time before jaded was a possibility,
when you'd hear of a neighbor's sister's cousin's friend dying
and you'd cry one tear like that one scene in *Glory*
when Denzel manages to drip pain and still look strong.
Back when Bambi's mother dying was the saddest thing in cinema
until you saw *The Lion King*,
when you still buried all of your dead fish,
thought that 911 would return to your neighborhood,
when you believed the singular purpose of chalk
was to outstretch a game of hopscotch,
when you felt shit all the way.

For me, it ended at nine.
Hot summer and my mother pours me
into the Powell Street BART station.
In my family, the East Bay meant food
so I was anticipating fried chicken,
but then I saw her—
ghostly and vacant, she stared right through me.
So I flashed her the biggest little girl smile I could,
all teeth, but I was losing the magic that children
carry in their smiles, the kind that can temporarily
relieve adult suffering.

My body was betraying me with its growth
and I just hope I was pretty
'cause I was the last thing she saw as she dove,
body to rail,
and I heard it,
Richmond train approaching
and she splattered across all the pages of my
nine-year-old memory like cum on vintage Playboys,
never to be opened again between pages 48-52—
stuck.

I only open this shit when
absolutely necessary.

On days when life and death don't seem that far away
from each other and I question choosing life,
I see her face and cry.
Sometimes pain is your only indicator that you're still ticking,
and sometimes death reminds you how the fuck to live.

See, in a country where we write songs
about blood-splattered flags
in the dawn's early light,
and then re-sing them for everything
from funerals to baseball games,
does death even faze you?

And if it doesn't,
have you convinced yourself you're living all the way?

Alley Cat

Dedicated to Jenessa Ferrell and Jamon Schlafke[1] and Cassandra Cardona

Regarding teen parenting by a recovering teen mother:

1.
I have always imagined alley cats know they are alley cats
know their young will not be presented in baskets with bows
for Christmas
know that scavenging is less hobby than need.

I have always imagined the alley cat knows well that the world
wants it to hide and in this way I have always known I was
an alley cat.

2.
Society so often gives me opportunities to be sorry,
I sometimes lose track of the span of my mistake
mistake my frame for a statistic that will not see bell curve.
The world has taught me well about how I fucked up
I mean how I'm a fuck-up,
how I needed prevention
I mean how I'm worth preventing,
how I need resource
I mean how I drain the system.
The world has a lot to say.

3.
Meet Jamon, sixteen, part-time employee
of the Boys & Girls Club, mentor, student, brother, son, friend.
Meet Janessa, thirteen, published artist, sister, daughter, friend.
Two kittens worthy of bows
two answered prayers
two alley cats who know how to hide.
I gave you their credentials first 'cause that's what we do here
in this caste system,
and as a peasant who self-affirms Queen I know well how
to play the game.

---

1 Inspired by Sonya Renee Taylor and The Body Is Not an Apology movement

4.
I apologize for the following:
There is a sixteen-year-old girl who sometimes crawls
out of my throat
angry with the way I buried her as a child,
a child with no tact, just reaction,
whose tongue is a sword
who never a lot of things.
The world has imparted that this is unique,
Emotional Immaturity,
that we teen mothers are the only ones with gaps in our
development but
there is a woman inside of me who raised herself,
who knows more about accountability than most
who baby rocks the sixteen-year-old to bed most nights
who wipes the sorry off her skin but never stops her
from saying it.

5.
I have long since desired to be able to tell my childrens' creation
story holy
tell them of the brave man I once met
the one with all the fishing line in his back,
how we underwater fell in love while the line was pulled daily,
how resilience isn't honored in America
but we too are American,
the adjectives in textbooks
the activity of dreams
how survival is an art our family knows well.

6.
I am fighting the urge to give you my testimony;
the urge to explain how many times I opened my legs as a child,
the lure of victim,
for I was taught to prove how pure I still am,
so in this moment see me as whore
as fatherless child
as craving
as fiend
as void
as lost
as stupid
as naive
as bad-boy chasing
as giver of everything
and hear loudly I am worthy.
Hear loudly of my striped belly bearing evidence of its young.
Hear loudly!

7.
Things I am not sorry for:
Applying for and using
Food stamps
Cash aid
WIC
Medical
Rental Assistance
Going to food pantries
Living in poverty
For the part of me that is all stereotype
For this poem.

8.
A stanza for women:
This body sprouts woman faster than child wants blooming
but girl and woman both are flower
Pollen and Queen
ecosystem foundation
breath force of the forest
the city
the town.
The body sprouts woman faster than environment sprouts support
beehive bustling frame woman
resilient fragrant thing.
The body is not sin,
all of creation closer than breath
life singing hymns through your skin.
You are answered prayer.
You are sanctuary.
You are home.
You are mother.
You can't help but be holy.

9.
For our children:
Alley cats are smarter than pets,
more resourceful
more brave.
Your mother never meant you burden,
never meant you shame,
never meant you bowless,
But she did mean you animal
Be animal.

Credit to Robin "Mama" Lerios

Jasmine, Janessa, and Jamon
Credit to Valerie Schlafke

Universe Dust

I am woman, so expect me to bring home the bacon.
Shit, expect me to rule the whole fucking world.
Sometimes you will remember me as man, so assume
I will throw down in the kitchen,
be consistent enough to sing lullabies.
I am two stories simultaneously playing,
and I am quite comfortable being both.
This is not to say I identify as man
but most Black women know what it is
to have this kind of strength reinforced.
Single mothers whisper the stories of their manhood
when folding feminine will prevent forward movement
through the struggle,
and queer women all over the world know what it is
to be ripped of their aprons and lace!
I need to write a piece
dedicated to my still steady need to papel picado bleed
rainbows onto all of my whites.
Narcissism's best intentions,
a byproduct of nomadic travel,
this is where I am unashamed
to hail greet my German ancestry,
Jewish maternal traditions buried in the name of good old
American union.
This is where I first learned pride for soil I have never touched.
Jesse Owens right-fisted well beyond February-type shit.
See, identity work is a needed pathway towards actualization
like: I am actually here.
And existing by your own definition is powerful.
Before I splinter into Universe dust,
become the rolling waves yearning for the moon,
antes que estoy known as big mama stories,
and someone's request for really good advice,
while I still feel pretty fucking human
I need to write about me.

Credit to Alexandra "Little Dragon" Moskow

Credit to Raggedy Andey

Belly

After 30 seconds of choreographed heteronormative movement
he pulls away to hold my belly,
cradles any shame he senses in a visceral way
and refuses to stop
until I catch his eyes
until he feels breath land in this thing once a sewer,
until my chest flutters
and I cease impersonating statues,
until my hands are jealous of his for touching something so soft
so kind
so honest
so home,
until I let him in this home,
until my bark rambles about these trunk rings,
until my center is my center and my chakras
stop hiding magic from each other,
until I am ready to drum kit again
until I am music,
until my fat is the cake he gets when he finishes cake,
until I cry if needed because only so much water can live
in one being
until I start designing my next bikini,
until I am supple enough to unfold
to blossom
to lay down
to surrender
to top while playing bottom
until I know I have all the power
the thunder
the rain.
It does not matter how much I run away
he will breadcrumb find me
he will
breadcrumb find me.

Permission

You can dance on my body,
try your moves on my skin.
Here's your permission,
I'll let you in.
Welcome to my Yes because the wrath of my 16-year-old No
not yelled loud enough still haunts my
nightmares from repeating and I don't wanna scare you.
My Yes is so much more welcoming—
oh, and welcome you are, too.
Red carpet shaped like woman in no way for walking
and talking is optional.
I'd like to spit at you in sweat and instinct,
sing with the melodic shaking of thighs,
scream out yes, yes, yes
all while biting my lower lip in reservation
like let me save some of this please,
bent on my knees and receiving, change the rhythm of my breathing
and know you are welcome.
Slide your fingers into creation and let this be our meeting place,
and just in case you are still curious, you are welcome.
Welcome, notice how satisfaction can be found
when our lips meet,
how praise can be offered while panting with flexed feet
and oh I do worship our safety,
how my No could revisit and you would gladly meet it
white flag and fully surrendered
blue from a lack of release,
how there's no hiding the crease my belly provides
and who hides when it's our nature to explore.
You make me feel
like the holiest of whores.
You can dance on my body,
try your moves on my skin.
Here's your permission,
I'll let you in.

Artwork by Marissa "Moose" Morales

Love Letters to My Limbs

Dear Thighs,

You are whispering of womanhood and your chant is alluring.
The diamond-shaped light spewing from your center tip-top
the dimples flirting with the fury of certain muscles,
all of you a prayer.
You are the reason hip-hop started using the word *juicy* again.
A thank-you of a limb.
Altar of fertility,
how your slope is set on descending,
how I fall in love with you, thick resilience.
Womanhood as home.
You are rubbing the sound of creation back into the ground.

Love,
Jasmine

Dear Arms,

How you sweep the making of wings near your crown
ripple with rivers on your territory
–and they call them stretch marks!
You sing story
give thanks!
For I have carried,
I have dropped,
I have held
you hymn of holy landscape.
Praise be all of you
wrist to valley and then again
how you sweep the making of wings near your crown.

Amen

Interview 1
Interview by Rylan Freshour

When did you start writing poetry?
Privately, around 10. I started writing hooks for hip-hop songs and love letters. The occasional angry rant about being young.

When did you start taking it seriously?
It wasn't until 2008, when I tried out for slam.

Had you been writing in between then?
My writing had always been a spiritual practice, a place to go when I felt alone. A place for me to think new thoughts and transform pain.

How many notebooks do you have?
I probably have thirty-something notebooks.

What made you try out for slam?
I finally realized that my voice was unique, that my story wasn't one that was told a lot, and that people needed to hear it. I also realized that it could be a healing act to talk about my darkest hour in a celebratory space.

Why is it important that people hear your story?
Particularly my story around mental health is one that isn't often written about from a firsthand perspective. Because of that I think it's imperative that narrative exists.

What do people need to understand about mental health issues that they don't?
Behind the diagnosis is a human who has a story that can't be told universally. The more stories shared, the more we have an understanding of how to thrive and live with mental disabilities.
I think people think of functional mentally disabled people as inherently different from someone screaming on a street corner, but in my experience such a line is very, very blurry. How do you see that difference, if there is one. In most ways I do not see a

difference because in my body, at any given point, I can be close to psychosis if I don't take care of myself. So I try to remember that the guy yelling at himself in the middle of traffic, or the homeless woman talking to herself in the grocery store, is just like me. The distinction for me is the willingness to practice consistent care, be it through a pharmaceutical or Earth-based approach.

That's a hard choice to make, especially in the middle of psychosis. How did you make it?
It was post-psychosis, really. The crisis of my lack of balance had climaxed, and I realized I wanted more ease. I made a commitment to take my pills for a year and see if it made a difference. It did, so I continued.

Where do you think you would be if you hadn't?
There's no telling really. I survived many years without it.

Would you say writing this book is an evolution of your recovery?
Yeah, to a certain degree. There is a redemptive aspect to sharing these poems. I needed to articulate my survival.

Affirmation for Coronation

I am a worthy human temple,
a place for good to operate from.
Justice is meant to radiate through me,
this and more is true by birthright.

My sexuality is sacred, fluid, and mine.
I give permission to myself to take full power of my body
again and again.
I give permission for my body to be a place of conscious healing.
Imperfect, perfection; curated by the Creator.

My history is evidence of my strength.
In fact, my testimony powers my journey.
Transcendance
Courage
Humanity
Endurance
Authenticity
Beauty
Forgiveness
and LOVE I am.

I am alive to my essence once again.
I am a worthy temple.
I AM just as I am.
Amen
Ashe
And So It Is

Credit to Katie Roper

II
Why I'm Crazy

To my beloveds,
Jamon, Janessa
To my revolutionary mother,
Valeria Schlafke

Prayer for Why I'm Crazy

Creator
this day I bring my broken, desiring to know I was made of your wholeness.
I bring my big feelings,
the abstract painting inside of me I have no words for,
the shame of being broken and flawed.
Today God I offer you my crazy and claim groundedness.
Today I offer you my best thinking and claim peace.
Today I remember once again that you restored a right spirit inside of me and that I am your child.
I claim my birthright.
Thank you for the opportunity in compassion depression is.
Thank you for the opportunity in transcendence my chemistry is.
Thank you for the lesson in oneness you teach me daily.
I am blessed right now in you.
And So It Is
Amen
Ashe

In the Body

I lived my first nine years all the way in my body
but relocated to the space above my neck by ten.
Overloaded and non-visceral
from my crown to the filter in my neck
I would eventually look into leasing
the space near my heart out again.
In time I'd fall in love
deep breathe drop past lungs into gut
and this was scary,
to feel fluttering behind the stone barriers I had worked so hard
to build.
This was humbling
to admit the linoleum over hardwood mistake I made in
disconnection
Living in your body is not as easy as it sounds.
Watch…
twist your hips
dance like you fittin' to get it on.
Does that make you uncomfortable?
If so, when did that begin?
Suck in your stomach.
Now let it bloat.
Are you scared someone will see the bulge?
Was sucking in more comfortable?
How many times have you looked in the mirror today?
And when you did, did you tell the truth with your eyes?
Your body wants to answer all these questions.
See, I am slightly nervous,
something akin to first-kiss jitters is dancing right on my center
my back is tight with money issues
and my chest is loose enough to accept the air
I peekaboo hide my middle 'cause I am still healing.

And right here
someone close has severed themselves from themselves
in an attempt to evacuate a natural disaster;
they're still cleaning up Katrina.
Be careful about the unattended,
it only seems to grow and fester.
This is a disclaimer:
I don't want you to wake up from the bliss of orgasm
pleasure to panic
in mid-teleport travel back to your childhood room
screaming at your now-chosen lover.
It can happen, believe me.
Instead, feel this,
the stretch of the plié,
and dream with me
of the last time you lived in your skin
from head to toe.
Yes, dream yourself all the way nine,
or whatever age it was when you lived true to your design.

Bipolar 1: Dear Mom

While the hospital bracelets still look fresh against my weary
skin, my mother asks me what it feels like to be bipolar.

This is a type of coming out of the closet I will always resent.
I want to tell her the best parts first so I tell her
it's magic carpets when you fall in love,
music in the body electric hymns expelling even through
fingertips, just how spacious big can be
how much I get to love her.
With horror in her eyes she leans in and asks:
"That's the manic part, right?!"

No.

For those of us forced to share our most beautiful features
under glass,
imagined ourselves museum exhibits grateful for the patrons
even while they wear us down,
for synapse-delayed reactors
with wide vision and big feelings,
when someone asks you what it feels like to be bipolar
make sure they have room enough for your answer.

See, my mother wasn't ready for the details,
how the first time I fell in love I held him so close
I could see all his secrets,
watched his brother force his mouth open
for secret kisses in secret places,
watched him harden his shell ritualistically.

See, mysticism and intuition do not always detour to avoid hell.
Mama, are you sure you're ready?
It's a lot to understand what good friends I've made with suffering,
how I fall down the beanstalk so often
I've now mastered hard soil landings.

Do you want to know my secrets?
How when my co-worker says to me:
"I don't even know how to lie"
I don't even know what she means.

Do you remember what it was when I was just your little girl?
The fiercest part of your spirit amplified.
Do you remember talking with friends, taking guesses at what I might become
a doctor, a lawyer, a minister...
me dancing all the while, pretending not to hear the compliments.

See, being bipolar is just like that but there are no compliments.

It's watching circles of your kin postulate your future's limitations and pretending not to hear.

I cannot help that my father's liquids hiss and froth with yours
like baking soda and vinegar,
nor that I am that bitter-tasting explosion.
I love you big,

unbalanced through both sides of this closet door.
I will never know if you will understand what it feels like
to be bipolar,

but I have always prayed that you would die remembering
what it was to love someone crazy.

Bipolar 2: Dear Children

Dear children,
you will hear them talk of me
brown, broke, and in need.
You will hear them calculate my odds over and over.
Remember how science works,
my diagnosis doesn't erase my title as your mother.
I am not terribly unique, so remember how crazy cradles
comfort in our home
remember crazy as your provider
remember how science works
all you need is an educated guess
choose your own hypothesis.
I'm gonna stop myself now,
'cause this wasn't meant to be pep talk.

This is how I share with you things I can't say yet.

Six weeks ago when you stayed with Toni
and Mom went to the hospital
she had made a choice not to take her medicine
or to sleep
or eat much
while you were both with your father.

See (speaking in the third person calms me down 'cause this is scary),
I was not suicidal,
I was angry,
$5.00-in-the-curse-jar kind of pissed.
Police car to the Behavior Health Unit
and when I arrived… well, if you ever have questions…

Perhaps it would be more productive to begin answering questions now.

Do I hear voices? Kind of.
Poetry sings to me in the midnight hour
undresses my confusion to reveal clarity
and she, has, quite, the, range.

Do I talk to myself? Yes, all the time.
So does everyone.
Us humans are just taught silly ways to pretend that isn't true.

Would I ever kill myself? No, but I know that sort of pain.
Did I ever try to kill myself while you were alive?
It was raining and you both were with your father
I took as many pills as I heard raindrops
until I saw your finger traces red, yellow, and blue plastered on preschool paper.
You are both my primary colors.

You guys saved me and that's not all the way okay,
because living for others isn't enough to stay all the way alive,
and primary colors aren't enough to make a rainbow.
You will hear them speak of me.

Do not listen to lies.

Bipolar 3: Dear Lovers

Dear Lovers,
you will hear of me broken, yet sleep with the whole woman.
Practice remembering the music my curves sing,
remembering me as orchestra
for I am sure not to share music all the time.
People will explain me in rhythms you haven't yet heard
explain me staccato
simple beats become seducing
remember how I change

Shift
Dance
remember me fluid like something you loved to hear
you will have opportunities to do all of this slowly.
Groove us
Music

I'm sorry now, before "I'm sorry for us" needs to happen.
I forgive me now before "I'm sorry" needs to happen.
I forgive you now before "I'm sorry" needs to be said.
I would love to dance with you, just ask.
I'm pretty good on my feet, good shoes or not,
pretty quick to join a cipher without a beatbox.
I told my children I am the same woman in all spaces—
this will confuse you as much as it confuses them.
I really AM though
All spaces.

When your handling learns my song
really make new
music itself,
remember when we have
remember our Pit Pat
for thunder is inevitable,
the earth will shake with things to say.

Who's making the music?
Come on poet.
Come on dancer, come on artist.
What do you know about me?
About us?

Hold what you know
like it was the rhythm that kept this song going,
and I'll remember you in kisses
in long hugs
in Sundays and rocking chairs.
I remember how the wind blows before we sing,
how cool it feels on the dance floor before we move.
I remember everything.

Sincerely,
Me
Queen, Peasant, Healer of your choosing
of your whisper
of your want
Amen

Underwater

While underwater I somehow still could breathe
through the muffled wall psychosis constructs during
sleepless nights,
the candy elixir of mania on my tongue
the rushed air of the train that's coming,
how I can't help but be its station,
and my observer standing on the last piece of dry land inside of me
restricted to its perch while waves cover my territory.

Jasmine, watch Jasmine
shed her clothes in parts in public,
draw on her walls in broken script,
send messages that don't make sense to people who
don't make sense,
give away her belongings as though she has enough to give,
speak in rage only,
not sleep for days without drugs,
kiss the wrong lips,
trust the wrong folks,
starve her failed frame,
divorce her hygiene practices,
walk barefoot on broken glass.

Jasmine, watch Jasmine be a drug
the architecture of destruction,
tsunami her humanity
for her village.

This is not treading water;
I am submerged in watching others watch me,
brace myself for the moments my support network
will never forget
slow motion watch the drop of their jaws
the face of how impossible they see me in this moment,
the freeze frame I will forever now see in their eyes when they
look at me.

To touch so intimately the line drawn on condition by those
who love me most
to see the sea and everything it screams
the present and the past making out in front of me,
teasing me with their sounds
their memories
their stamp.

How the ocean can hold it all.
How no human can.
How I feel like my own ocean
rip tide pulling me away from myself
toes now drenched on my dry perch.
I am activity of expectation and surprise all at once.
Stigma just like stereotypes are birthed from something
in these moments I am that something,
I am gone to them now and just water.

My old Reverend told me once that all of my poems should
come full circle
that I should never leave my listeners in hell
—advice that almost stopped this poem from being born.
The truth is hell has been perfectly within my reach some days.
Truth is when things are drenched they take a while to dry out,
they are prone to mold and fungus.
I am sometimes still damp.
I will always bear the evidence of saltwater on my skin
and maintenance means buoyancy only on good days.

Hell and heaven have to make friends inside of me if I'm ever to
travel on land again.

There is a prayer in my gut somewhere hoping my listeners still can
spell heaven with my words, still can see beach days in my smile.
May that be so because they know I'm an ocean
as below, so above,

because they are proud of the way I've dried off.
May that be so because nothing is in vain
not even the climax of my movie
not even my visceral memory of shame
not even my ugly
my nightmare.

For in the end I breathed through all of it somehow.
For in the end I am still breathing.

Recipe

Here is the recipe I'm currently recommending
for healing patterns of white supremacy, racism, and privilege.
Since these are ongoing dialogues this recipe is not complete,
in fact, that is your first ingredient—
one part knowing that there is no done
no complete
no badge
no certificate. Add to your life
the ability to fuck up gracefully,
say sorry without defending
listen more than talk
hear the sound of your own voice saying I don't know over and
over again until humility forms a new
muscle in your mouth.

Why you always looking at me for a recipe?
Why you always reducing my blood into food worth dissecting
for study?
Why is this simple formula the easiest way to tell you what I need?
Victory can feel sad,
can feel like a broken gift
as we are broken in our words
broken in our training
as we are human.

Offer something
add something
do something
like read a shitload of articles and be available for a revelation
like read a shitload of articles and not need every time to
validate your good job at reading through
me
like attend a workshop
like whatever it is white people need in this process

like white people are a worthy people worthy of a process
add something on your own because silence has had its way with you too long
because not knowing so much makes you move
because evolution in your DNA has led you forward.

Finish this poem.

The Black Body

Whereas the body is a temple,
the Black Body is a temple burning vacated before worship most days,
a structure too often in motion to complain about its architecture.
Let's face it
ain't many whiny motherfuckers got Black Bodies
and most of us
have an uncle whose knees swell with the moon,
who will never tell his nerve narratives to his doctor,
an aunty with the "sugars" and hypertension
who will grasp at her chest silently over freshly cooked southern food
and can't many imagine complaining about pain as hobby,
as though there is an invisible auction block swinging over our heads
reminding us our bounty is only good while strong and lean.

May 29, 2013
I am arrested for bouncing a check.
—clearly another poem altogether—
Six of us hold together the ritual of being held captive in a van,
Three of us complain with every twist, turn, bump,
Three of us take it,
like slavery is genetic.
See, this is also ritual.

June 2006
The doctor says it takes six to twelve gallstones to be eligible for surgery.
He looks at my center with sound-making faces he clearly did not learn in medical school:
"You have 121, Jasmine."
How much pain can you hold?

July 1989
The first lady of the First Baptist Church
with the shiny skin and good hair
says she "didn't even know I was mixed on account of how strong I was."
That "Black woman can take pain,"
that I am "growing into a Black woman just fine,"
how far back does this go?

See, the Black Body is a time capsule with a consistent story,
a weed that knows what it is to surface through concrete
and still survive.
So here is a prayer for the burning temple:

Blessed be the Black Body,
these melanin memories that know strength in this way
worthy of touch, of healing, of release.
Blessed be the bones scattered in the Atlantic in triangles,
the captive Black Body all locked up and everywhere to go,
the frail Black Body beating all statistics available,
the newborn Black Body just available,
worthy of touch, of healing, of release
Amen
Ashe
And So It Is

Yemaya

The first Mekka was the Ogun River
It was here that Nigeria would bless fertility
Baptise Black skin in the name of the earth
Her container was big enough to hold her name's meaning there
Mother whose children are fish
She was a sufficient ecosystem to nurse her young
And we all were her young
This was the shape of her before trespass
Before ships would sail toward her land with thirst
Hungry for her fish
But the day the chains touched her earth
The day slavery severed the spiritual truth of freedom
She would learn to leap herself into an ocean
Learn to be big enough to hold the grief birthed from such things
She sang to her children boarded and chained
With every crashing wave
Salt-stained impression
She would bellow
I am still here
She sent her sharks off to follow the ships
Taught them to consume her children like fish when they jumped off into her arms
Knew that the pain inflicted would have nothing on the pain already endured
One by one Black women would leave themselves like bread on the path of the Atlantic Sea floor
Scream in their silence their faith in the mother above all
One by one they would scream aloud for their true master
Those on board never able to forget their shreel
Their shreel the soundtrack for the breach made to her riverbed
The stories of their bones would travel back to land
Weave themselves into sentences about bravery
This was not suicide
Suicide in the context of slavery does not exist

To this day
The loudest of sounds the ocean makes
are the ones of rattling bones and mothers' cries
Africans unwilling to be slaves
Foremothers with Africa still on their tongues
Reminding the slave in us we once were free
Yemaya licks the borders of our land in rhythm with the moon
Still the loudest lullaby we know

Black women have not lost the ship diver in their eyes
The freedom in their glare even in the most captive of places
Still barter which threat is worse
the chain or shark
Black women still find themselves told aloud as brave
And in some way always are dying
Always reaching for something bigger to trust than what's given
Never has much been given
She lost more sons than most years
Was thrown Black-fleshed children by the handfuls in truth
The whip turned cuff some seasons ago
And I swear she is plotting to leap again
To devour her own fish children in the name of becoming
a riverbed
To floor rest all the chains
Submit to the cries of the foremothers
Black women have not lost the ship diver in their eyes
and in this way time does not exist
More so there is one stare she gives
that says I have learned to hold everything
Learned to bed silt and salt both
Learned to summon my own freedom when chained
A stare that swells with an entire ocean behind it
that says
I have never been afraid to jump

Affirmation for Why I'm Crazy

My darkness is never void of light
A right spirit resides within me.
I am always within a possible walk towards balance
I am always radiating life.
Wholeness
Celebration
Health.

There is nothing wrong with me.
The struggle is real and resides within God,
Poverty is not my fault.
within possibility.

I am possible.
I am possible.
I am possible.

Self-love is a revolutionary act.
I am revolutionary.
Today I'm crazy
Resilient
Crazy brilliant
Crazy healing
Crazy alive
and Crazy needed.
Amen

Credit to Alyssa Young

III
Kinship

To the resilient Kara Bobila

Prayer for Kinship

Oh Lord: Self-existent one
thank you for the words friends provide
how they spill out safety sometimes
for the lessons only learned in community
the stretch and pull of reflective expressions
for their face as you.

Oh Lord I can't box up as man only,
thank you for how you hold me in my kin's arms
for how the ancestors have passed down this ability
to cultivate kinship,
for the student I am in teaching,
the pupil I am in leadership,
the daughter I am in your care.

Bless this day my homies
their survival
their full thriving,
Thank you for the opportunity of growth through community
in my life,
bless this day my family
as I know we are one
the way you allow me to heal in family daily
for my chosen family
for my family of origin,
for the way all those people are my teachers,
for the moments that I am.
for poets who are invested in my work,
for healers with a yes to show up for my life,
for sisters, brothers, cousins, and more,
for opportunities to show up for them.
Gratitude is my prayer.
And So It Is
Amen
Ashe

Rest in Peace, Pete McLaughlin
  [Art Bar]

My Friend

Queen Jasmeen and Raggedy Andey

READING KEY
Regular text = Queen Jasmeen
Italics = Raggedy Andey
Bold = Together

I know her greatest fears
I know her greatest accomplishments are her children
How often she dyes her hair
what sort of ingredients she likes to cook meals with
But it took getting onto a slam team for us to ever share our rape stories
We have no practice for such storytelling
So we wing it

She recites the story first by stating facts
Her age
The location
Not his name though
facts: her skirt, its buttons, the door she used to sneak out.
when she says "sneak out," the dip in her voice asks me to recognize this
as some sort of culpability.
that i am to know it is this place in the story where i hold her accountable,
even just a little bit.
As she pulls for language to narrate the memory movie she is clearly watching
She finds my eyes only to explain that she doesn't remember saying no
That she remembers her father saying
"never let him hit you"
but never learned how to stop a man from forcing himself inside of her

watch the porcelain in us shatter
We anticipate this damage
and the main emotion she remembers was the finality of it all
like "well it had to happen sometime and at least now it's over"
she tells me she doesn't remember lying down
just the rocks that embedded themselves in her
producing bruises to later serve as the only outward evidence of her war
she swims through the liquid in the story to get to me, she names them as she goes:
sweat, sweat, sweat, and cum.
my friend gets to me,
defeated. her body looking smaller than usual,
the whole frame of her caving on itself.
Her bones all seek to rip out of her skin
To build some new sanctuary
Her veins all sing revenge aloud
Courting the adrenaline we all wish we would have had
My friend is a different kind of angry today
The kind we reserve for God
Survivors don't share their stories for a reason
We are too scared the wars trapped inside of us could kill again
The world has taught us to play dead so well

That even poets stutter and go blank
What is it about our culture that teaches us that the rape story should dig out a space to live inside the victim?
What is it about rape and its silent direction for more silence?
I swear I know everything about her
But when she tells me her story
I meet a new part of her for the first time
I meet that piece of her she was told to bury, hide, and forget
I meet her distress head-on in the shape of back-to-back cigarettes
I swear I know everything about her
But today I learn the litany of untold stories each survivor holds within them
Today I learn how to hold my friend's tale and share the weight of my own.

Queen and Raggedy
Photo by Raggedy Andey

Enough

Queen Jasmeen and Raggedy Andey

READING KEY
Regular text = Queen Jasmeen
Italics = Raggedy Andey

My visible ribs are not an invitation to talk about my visible ribs. My silhouette not being truck-flap digestible is not an invitation to talk shit.

I eat at restaurants where I know there will be no leftovers. Like the carrying of the to-go box turns my person into a billboard that screams "I failed again. I didn't eat enough. I'm not enough." This same box will greet me later and repulse me regardless of its contents, it is a billboard that screams "Everyone else got this right the first time. Eat me, or fucking throw me away. Just hide the evidence of your not-enoughness."

It's expected I devour the plate,
expected my eating is less about nourishment and more about consumption
as though I have no "full"
no "stop"
no "wait,"
as though I am always empty for foods filling
a storage bin for gluttony.

To be full and fat is to be a liar,
talented at the art of pretending,
who all the while will eat alone in excess as expected.
I am careful what I wear. Careful not to show the stark outline of my skeleton too unashamedly or they will wonder how this being is sustained. They will watch me when I eat to make sure I do, they will pinch my thigh, pick me up, reduce me while chanting "lucky lucky lucky."

On the rare hot dates when I feel brave enough to let the world see my arms
I am careful not to stretch
not to take up too much space
careful not to catch the faces of disgusted women who fixate on my fat from the corner of their eyes
I am more careful than I should have to be.
Shopping for jeans that don't make me look like the 13-year-old boy that I DO look like, and a group of women in Forever 21 busy their mouths with "bitch, lucky, slut, skinny" while their eyes devour my frame as it involuntarily puffs itself up like a bird with plumage armor. There is no place to hide from any of their regurgitated programmed hatred in a body that was already deemed to not be enough by the lack of size zero jeans while all their ads advertise women HALF my size.
Their eyes say you're in the wrong store
and trust me, thumbing through reminders that I can't fit this world
size 0 to
not you
not now
not here
is not my pastime of choice.

How to disappear effectively in Forever 21:
Travel the rim of the store close enough to step out at all times,
Effectively scan the sale items quick enough to slip in and out of the few large options remaining,
Look at shoes,
always shoes,
only shoes,
Pay quickly,
Be swift
Be forgotten.

When I speak about this with you (Jasmine) I catch little distinctions in my own dialogue. I call you a "woman" and myself a "girl." How much of our own fabric still has the threads of their brainwashing woven through it?

When are we both allowed to just be, enough?

In California

Queen Jasmeen and Gabriel Kittle-Cervine

READING KEY
Regular text = Queen Jasmeen
Italics = Gabriel Kittle-Cervine
Bold text = Together

In California the ocean paints the illusion of freedom down the coastline
washing over all the memories we'd rather not talk about
In California when a white man says nigger at an open mic in a "progressive" beach town
The polite thing to do is to *say nothing*
Small talk about how ridiculous it was later behind their back
And show others at some point that *I was appalled*
In California when a white man says nigger it is called into question whether
saying anything about it is *"infringing on freedom of speech"*
or that *"it's really a matter of censorship"*
phrases like *"that wasn't the intent"* and *"it's relevant when put into context"* are thrown out as if to imply there's a nice way to say it
In California action is most easily stirred when noise is made and the internet is alerted
When a Black girl yells loud enough to fuck up your Facebook feed
When a White boy stays silent long enough to lose faith in his own ability to be an ally
When silence gets too hard to hold inside all the witnesses
When they are made to admit their own refrain from action aloud
When he said it, I didn't say anything, I didn't approach him, I bit my tongue instead of his
When demonizing the man who spoke the word tires itself out and is exposed as **just another way to not be accountable**

we offer our silence to sea and make postcards of all the things we **do not say**
In California gentrification has cleaned up anything plantation-inspired long ago
and we are good at believing that western expansion makes us some kind of **utopian ideal for multiculturalism**
manufacturing a myth of the American Dream to hide the genocide they were committing
In California a Black girl learns that liberals are not to be mistaken with allies
That allies do most of their work in the dark
That liberals just want to not fuck up and get some credit for it
That there is no equivalent word to show the sunny state of how nigger stings
That white people keep trying to relate to what she has gone through
instead of respecting her right to **live without the expectation of being both lesson and teacher**
That it is only healthy for her to assume that her white friends know her as nigger somewhere in the back of their minds
That no matter how much i claim to be an ally
i still unintentionally tokenize her
abuse my privilege and never even notice
using shame and guilt as an excuse for being problematic
In California the same girl is called
"Over-reactive"
"Dramatic"
"Sensitive"
Accused of
"Not being community-focused"
Black girl visits herself as island
Learns to master alone while in the company of others
Takes space because she cannot house nigger a smile quick enough to please California
Is reminded the only way to say pain in Black is angry

In California we believe the ocean can absolve us of any guilt
We believe that racism is wrong, *especially in public*
That Black girls are free
That niggers are free
That liberals are down
That poets are conscious
In California we whisper in silent activism and act like it's enough
we hope our dependence on racism will wash away with the waves
but the tide always returns fog-thick with our complacency
In California silence is the easiest word to speak
while still being politically correct
and we speak it
well.

Interview 2

Interview by Rylan Freshour

Do you think there is a connection between mental illness and creativity?
In my body, the two are friends who communicate regularly.

For you it's a collaborative process within yourself?
I have never known a separation between them; crazy and art come from a similar intuitive place in my skin.

Do you feel like your art is related to how you perceive life?
I perceive art first, then life, on a good day.

Is life a side effect of art?
Life is art.

Is living life as a person with mental illness like making art as someone with mental illness?
On a good day, yes.

How would you characterize your art on more together days and less together days?
I can show up as anything from tsunami to meadow.

Which do you prefer, tsunami or meadow?
I like meadows, whereas tsunamis aren't forgotten.

You told me a famous comedian would go off his meds for his movies; do you ever do that for poetry?
No, not for poetry.

But you value the experiences you have had; do you use their memories in your poetry today?
They are the meat and potatoes of the meals I serve.

Do you feel like you are a different person when you experience psychotic episodes?
No, I am the same woman in all places even as I change.

I feel like when I have episodes I swing between being a jerk and someone who's depressed, and there's little of me in between. Do you experience that too?
I am working hard to sew together the many me's within me and remember my wholeness daily.

Do you use symbolism in your poems related to psychosis?
The metaphors I use feel real to me.

Meaning, you have experienced feeling those things?
My visceral memory of these things feel like metaphors.

So your memory is metaphorical, in a sense?
Kind of.

I have had experiences where I have temporarily seen reality through very changed eyes. Is that true for you?
It used to be, yes.

In those times, did you feel some kind of metaphorical reality?
No, it's only Western culture that has taught me to believe that the way I see is metaphorical.

Do you feel that you're a square peg trying to fit into a round hole that is Western society?
No, I feel like society likes to name me.

Is that because society is unprepared for the kind of perception you bring to the table?
Humans are more prepared for authenticity than we are taught to think.

I like to think of my memory as half-fiction. Do you feel the same way?
Not exactly.

Do you consider it to be all reality?
My own reality, yes.

Does your own reality match what society considers reality?
I don't give a fuck.

That's a healthy way to look at it. Have you always been that way?
Absolutely not.

You have consistently used your past, especially times where society would say you were less balanced, as inspiration for your work. Do you feel like you'll ever run out of inspiration?
In my mind, redemption and linear time have no relation; possibilities are endless.

You seem to have found peace with those times, but do you feel like you need redemption for them?
I don't know if I have found peace per se, but there is something redemptive in this healing work.

What has working on this book done for you?
It has reminded me that the phoenix can make use of its ashes.

Confinement Is Timeless

Queen Jasmeen and Chris 'L7' Cuadrado

Reading Key
Regular text = Queen Jasmeen
Italics = Chris 'L7' Cuadrado
Bold text = Together

These memories, this melanin
they must be Amerikkkan
no beginning and no end
aching to be free again.

Hard to complain really, my Brown ass didn't get
choked
shot
beaten
battered and
executed.
Eric Garner, Oscar Grant, Raul and Brisenia Flores, Andy Lopez

Red and blue flash in the rear view
glow reminiscent of torches in the hands of slave catchers.
The trauma imprinted in these cells of servitude,
shutdown survival mode
molecules mutate into malleable mass.
The body remembers these circumstances of pursuit
The muscles quaking with centuries of subjugation.
The flesh trembles in memories of massacre,
the already thin line between officer and overseer collapses into
occupier.
It becomes unclear whether or not you will live through this
encounter.
This time-traveling trauma teaches
us strategies of subordination as survival,
how to live on wounded knees
how to speak with severed tongues

how to exist knowing you may be abducted at any moment.

**But it's Hard to complain really,
my Brown ass made it out.**
Left with a taste of the infinite black bodies are facing all over America,
the repetitive lull of jail walls singing in my head at night.
42 hours might not have felt like long enough to warrant a poem
but check fraud is also known as feeding your young.
$127.00 dollars spent at COSTCO on the right night can mean strip search
Welcome to jail!
The bars all scream
Poverty has collided with your world and can't help but leave you a statistic
my development relies on ability to adapt to captive,
hold silently the instructions to slavery in my body language,
submit and surrender
and this is

Timeless

Timeless

*The way my body will fold under the authority of shackles in an instant.
The way my head knows to hang low in the presence of the overseers,
accustom itself to mush and slop served warm
familiar with empty calories and nutrient-deficient menus
fill out communal underwear with no complaint
open mouth, spread cheeks, with no reservation.
How I had already rehearsed the way I'd act if I ever got locked up.
How I grew up thinking it was only a matter of show time.
How my tongue bit itself when the guard called me a bitch.
How the chords of my neck slacked to a tension below resonance.
How there is a legacy of captive carved into our skin as if to read*
SLAVE.

Confinement is timeless.
Right now hundreds of thousands of bodies are captive while mine stands free.
It's hard to complain really.

These memories, this melanin
they must be Amerikkkan
no beginning and no end
aching to be free again.

Affirmation for Kinship

I am "not the ocean but a worthy drop"
a drop full of the everything I need to thrive,
my community is the ocean my life is supported by.
I nurture this gift.

I respect this gift.
I treat this gift as a gift.
I am "not the ocean but a worthy drop" of you, Goddess, I learn
to remember this through my village.
It is easy to see myself in their reflections.
Easy ain't the stuff our ancestors made us from
It is easy to see you in them.
so I celebrate the challenges that arise, I trust you God, work
with me to do my clearest thinking about the people in my life.
I trust that my community is part of your ecosystem and that
we are all connected.
I trust you in all ways.

We are not the ocean but worthy drops.

IV
Conclusion

She's Changing Me

*She's changing me,
she's changing me
expanding what I see.*

*She's changing me,
my God changing me,
knows me to be free
and my job is to "step not see the staircase."*

*My job is to cry and know I'm whole
and my job is to pray and purge illusion
and my job is to trust deep in my soul
that she's changing me
changing me,
knows me to be free.*

May this rain take the pain down gutters lined with alchemic possibility,
sweep years and fears into green vision,
pregnant buds will tease winter till spring comes and I will grow,
I choose to compost anything that still stings
re-meet it remade
savor fresh thought like rain,
appreciating shift 'cause it happens
even in the valley.
I can hear the whispers of the mountain tops
my territory's enlarged.

*She's changing me
expanding what I see.
She's changing me
love inside of me.*

May my growth not come with the bitter aftertaste of resentment.
Awkwardly beautiful, my shell casing breaks.
Feet and vines will take me where I need to go.
Change me.
Cease the wars waged by my own ego.
Every time I reach for the bars of a mind-made prison my spirit sings
I'm free though.
Teach me to love the unpracticed and unrehearsed.
Let the truest me burst through my former form completely
and Change Don't Come Neatly
so I'll be yours in disarray,
consistently practicing and will not stray
may my change come again and again this day.

www.ingramcontent.com/pod-product-compliance
Lightning Source LLC
Chambersburg PA
CBHW030456010526
44118CB00011B/958